Karen Frenkel

Published 2003 by Little Longstone Parish Meeting,
c/o Christmas Cottage, Little Longstone,
Derbyshire DE45 1NN, England
Telephone: +44 (0) 1629 640426
Email: michaelstuart@btinternet.com

Printed and bound by J.W. Northend Ltd.,
Clyde Road, Sheffield, S8 0TZ, England
Tel: +44 (0) 114 250 0331
Fax: +44 (0) 114 250 0676
Web site: www.northend.co.uk
Email: info@northend.co.uk
ISDN: +44 (0) 114 250 7814

The moral rights of the authors has been asserted.

All rights reserved. No part of this publication may be reproduced in any material form (including photocopying or storing it in any medium by electronic means and whether or not transiently or incidentally to some other publication) without the permission of the Copyright, Designs and Patents Act 1988 or under the terms of a licence issued by the Copyrighting Licensing Agency, 90 Tottenham Court Road, London W1P 9HE. Applications for the copyright owner's permission to reproduce any part of this publication should be addressed to the publisher.

A catalogue record of this book is available from the British Library.

ISBN: 0-9543 167-0-3

**Photograph on previous page: Little Longstone Congregational Chapel by Karen Frenkel.
Founded in 1844, the Chapel is still going strong.**

LITTLE LONGSTONE
INTO THE MILLENNIUM

Project Co-ordinator: Brian Edwards
Text: Michael Stuart
Principal Photographer: Karen Frenkel
Published By Little Longstone Parish Meeting

This book is an attempt to describe, in pictures and in words, the life and environment, today and yesterday, of the civil parish of Little Longstone, and has been produced as a result of a proposal by, and with the support of, the parish meeting and people of Little Longstone who wished to celebrate the New Millennium in some lasting way. Our thanks go to those people who encouraged us in many ways and enriched this book with their support.

Within the village we had a number of existing photographs but it was thought that additional professional expertise should be sought from outside. Karen Frenkel, a photographer from nearby Little Hucklow was thus commissioned to portray Little Longstone as it is today. We then set about coordinating her work with our pool of local illustrations.

Little Longstone is a small hamlet containing about one hundred inhabitants. To the north is the ridge of Longstone Edge, and there are magnificent views across and down the Wye valley, to Riber Castle and Crich Stand ten miles to the south, to the heights of Burton Moor and Sheldon across the valley to the southwest, whilst the iron-age hill fort of Fin Cop stands sentinel to the west. This volume is a celebration of the people, past and present, and of the history, buildings and landscape of the parish, in pictures and words.

There has never been a battle fought in the parish of Little Longstone, as far as we know, not even in the Civil War; the Yorkists and Lancastrians in the War of the Roses left it undisturbed, the paratroopers didn't land at nearby Great Hucklow as the Home Guard feared. Nobody born in Little Longstone ever achieved national or international fame or even reached the headlines of the Sun newspaper.

The history of Little Longstone is all about people, buildings and landscape, the buildings and walls they erected and used, the tracks and roads they travelled along, the fields they ploughed and mines they excavated, the quarries they dug into, but mainly the people; the ordinary folk because that's what they are, and also extraordinary for we are all unique and do extraordinary things. As one visitor put it, "the trouble with this village is it's full of eccentrics". Chambers Dictionary defines eccentrics as 'not conforming to common rules, odd'.

So this book is dedicated to the people of Little Longstone, those who were born here, those who lived here, and those who live here still.

The map opposite shows the roads and tracks in the parish, the line of the railway, and other salient features. The principal part of the village follows the line of Main Street between the Chapel and the Butts, but we must also include Monsal Head and the Dale as far as, but not including Cressbrook. It also emphasises how convoluted and illogical is the boundary between ourselves and our neighbours, so higgledy-piggledy in fact, that the mediaeval people, just to make sure they knew where they were, put a marker stone wherever the boundary met with a stone wall. The best example can be seen on Ashford Lane just below the Monsal Head Hotel (but mind the traffic, and you do have to look over the wall). Note the modern stone near the hotel entrance; the Longstone Bar is in Little Longstone (makes sense), the Stable Bar is in Ashford. The Monsal Head Café is completely in Little Longstone.

If you walk up the footpath signposted to Ashford from Monsal Head, you will see on the opposite side of the dale, on the slopes of Puttwell Hill, five or six rows of earth banks, called "lynchets", the remains of agricultural terracing, maybe 13th century in date, a

Karen Frenkel

View from Fin Cop across Monsal Dale and towards Cressbrook.

time when population explosion caused a demand for more farming land to feed hungry mouths. To the right is an old track, which, until 1866, was the road to Buxton, and may have been built by the Romans. Above the line of the hill, in the centre of the photograph, all that area from Upper Dale to the top of Hay Cop (the flat horizon to the right of centre), was used as farming land during Roman times; the fields are still there but only visible by aerial photography. The village, consisting of round houses and inhabited by native Celts, was just above the Upper Dale car park.

People have lived somewhere in our area for thousands of years. Around 15 prehistoric burial mounds have been found in the parish, mostly around Haytop and the Castlegate Lane. There, bodies of adults and children, along with flint tools, pottery and animal skeletons were found. Old Norse and Old English place names like Scratta and Lowe are to be found.

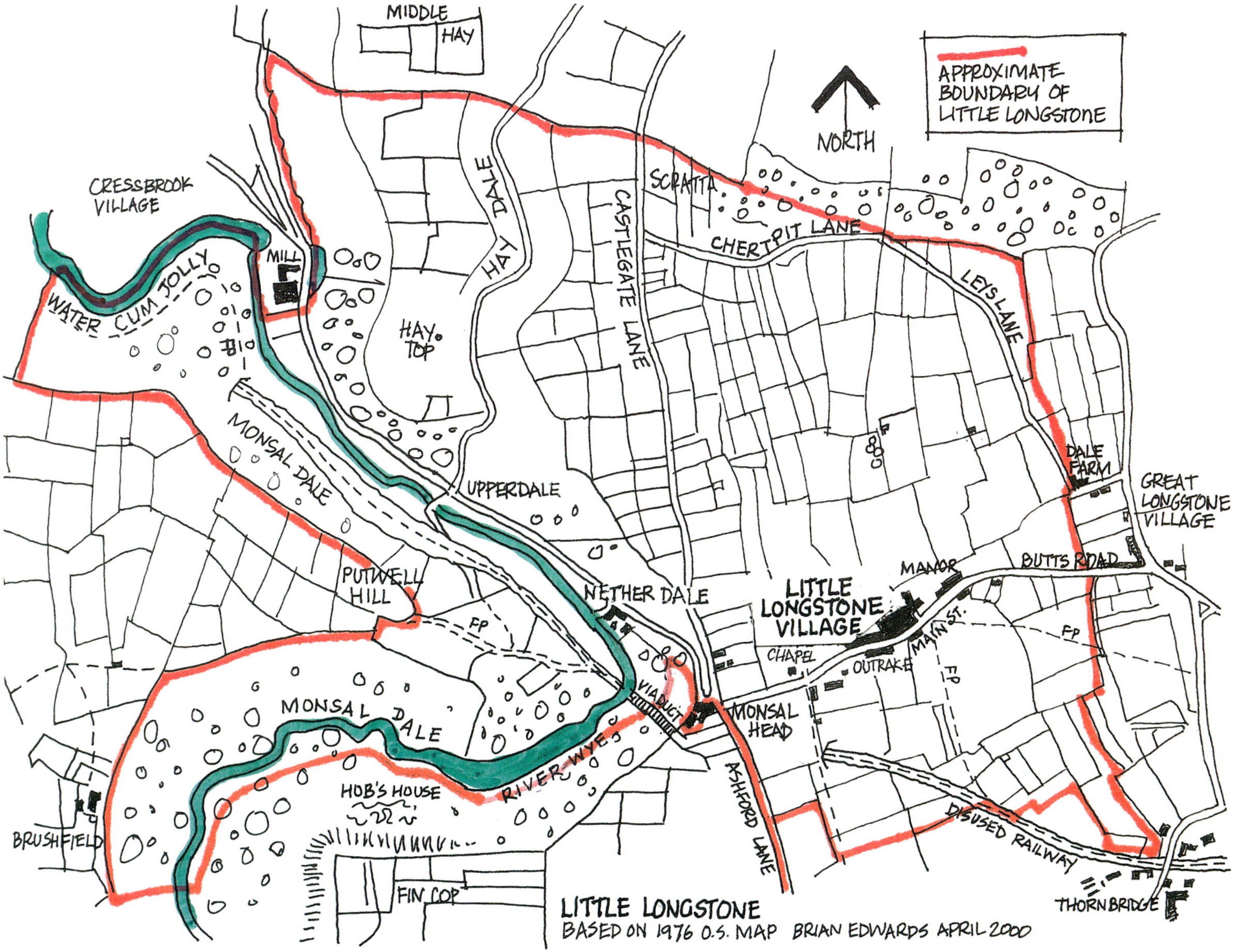

LITTLE LONGSTONE
BASED ON 1976 O.S. MAP BRIAN EDWARDS APRIL 2000

Peter Davey

A peaceful introduction to the village for many walkers is from the footpath that leads from Wardlow and Chert Pit Lane; Little Longstone is peeping out from amidst the trees.

LANDSCAPE

Wherever we walk or drive in the parish, we see the hand of people, countless generations of human beings who've made their mark on the landscape. The prehistoric peoples who chopped down the trees of what was then a countryside consisting mainly of woods and so prepared the ground for the first farmers, the Romans who brought a system of planned roads, the mediaeval husbandmen and lead-miners who marked out their particular property by building stone walls, and went on to use the same technology to replace their timber and wattle and daub houses and barns with stone walls. All these communities helped to make the landscape of today, and we, in our turn, are changing the home ground we inhabit to suit our requirements.

Lead mining and agriculture were not the only occupations in the village. Josiah Wedgewood (1730-1795) was a successful manufacturer of beautiful pottery, and a conscientious scientific experimenter, and it was only after rigorous trials that he decided that Derbyshire chert was the best material for grinding down flint, an essential ingredient of fine white china, and the name of Chert Pit Lane shows one of the sites where it was extracted (the quarry is now covered with trees).

1. Looking from Chert Pit Lane, towards Bakewell, with Stanton Moor on the far right, and Riber Castle in the centre.

2. Castlegate Lane. Roman soldiers once marched here, keeping the peace and organizing the natives, now it's Hulley's buses and speeding cars.

3. A misty morning from the Outrake, the railway marked by the line of trees in the foreground.

Karen Frenkel

Brian Edwards

Walter Adamson

Around Little Longstone you are never far away from sheep. Here the animals have appropriate thicknesses of coat!

8

Dick Richardson

Ray Manley

Jim on his dinky tractor doing the work of three dogs.

Having taken the lambs from their warm shed, he is now introducing them to the fields.

We don't need to point out that farming is the main traditional occupation of our area, although the number of workers involved is now a very small percentage of the population, or even the working population. Without agriculture, that is somebody doing something with the earth, we would not, perhaps, be living in such a beautiful, well-favoured (apart from the weather), part of our island. We now have only one farm, and one farmer, in the parish, although others come from outside to use our roads and fields, but it is worth remembering those buildings which were once upon a time, engaged in agriculture. Briary Dale, Leverets, Sunrise, Hollow and Ghurkha's Cottage, Meadow View, Holly Tree, Home Farm, The Stocks, Pear Tree, The Meadows, Longstone Byre, Quarters, Orr's Barn, and in Monsal Dale, Nether Dale, Riversdale, and Upper Dale, were all once farms or farm buildings.

Mary driving the tractor with Dan and Sarah helping as Jim loads the trailer with bales of hay, whilst elsewhere harvesting is under way and cows pose for the camera.

Jim is the last working farmer still living in the parish when once there were far more. Holly Tree was a poultry farm run by George Knowles, Leonard Timm kept cows at Meadow View, Harold Bacon used what is now Mary's stable, George Taylor farmed at Peartree, and the Oldfield family at Home Farm. (Frederick Oldfield had a daughter who was engaged for 35 years before she finally married the man of her dreams). There were three more farms down the dale.

Basically, this is grazing country, useful for fattening both cattle and sheep, although there aren't so many around after foot and mouth, but milking cows haven't been seen in the parish for many a long year.

Karen Frenkel

Some of the grazing land has now turned to scrub as seen here above Haydale.

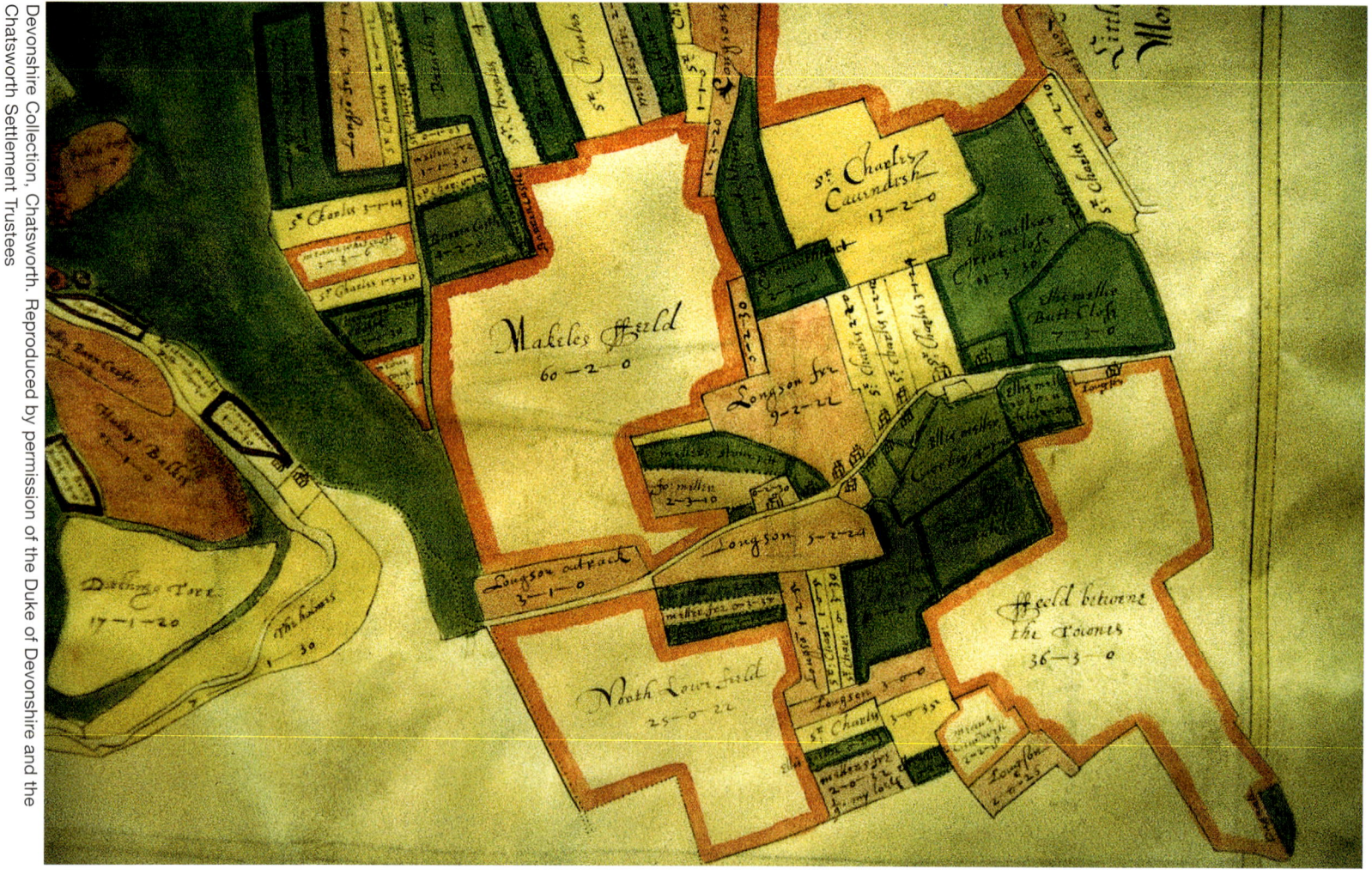

Devonshire Collection, Chatsworth. Reproduced by permission of the Duke of Devonshire and the Chatsworth Settlement Trustees

There is in Chatsworth a very beautiful map of Little Longstone, showing the fields and buildings, roads and rivers, all done in glowing reds, greens, yellows and browns, each field labelled with the area and the owner's name. The date is 1611, and the map clearly shows the remnants of the mediaeval three-field system. One of the names on the map is Hancock, and Alice Hancock died in 1634, owning goods worth £5 7s (£5.35p), a not inconsiderable sum in those days. Her late husband appears to have been a lead-miner as she owed a certain Humphrey Burrs twelve shillings (60p) for a load of lead ore. The poverty of some miners can be gauged from the will of William Bramall, died 1633; most of the household items he left were in a deplorable condition. The bed sheets were described as sorry and torn, the kitchen pans were worn to many holes, his wooden utensils were of small worth, and even his brass pot was taken by the bailiff, probably to pay a debt. His widow married again, a Robert Howson, also a miner, but even he was in debt, first to the Whites, Robert then Francis, then to Robert Clark, all three of them dealers in lead and living in Great Longstone. When John Bradbury died in 1639, Mr. Longsdon took a chest, a bed and a bench for one year's rent, which he claimed was owing to him. Nicholas Mellor in 1648 was owed £78 and a further £10 which was said to be "desperate", that is, unlikely to be ever re-paid. His son, also John, twenty years later, was owed over £160!!!

The first written records of Little Longstone refer to gifts of land which can't now be located, between men and sometimes women without surnames, who cannot be distinguished from other people having the same name, most of which can't be precisely dated although we are probably talking about the mid 1100s to the mid 1200s. One of those mentioned is Thomas, parson of Bakewell, who had at least two sons, Matthew and Richard, and it is most amusing to read those Victorian antiquaries who tried to explain with intricate circularity how a Catholic priest could also be a father of children.

Little Longstone was an agricultural community until the lead mines started up north of the River Wye in about the early 1400s.

The manor belonged to the Shackerley family of Cheshire until the Countess of Shrewsbury, otherwise Bess of Hardwick, bought it in 1597 and founded almshouses in Derby for eight men and four women, "poore aged and impotent persons", which was endowed by a rent of £100 on property held by her in Little Longstone.

Brian Edwards

Makeley's Pasture, which is just behind the chapel and referred to in the map opposite, was an open field in the Middle Ages, but is now criss-crossed by limestone walls erected when it was enclosed in 1824.

This Dutch Barn with fine arched openings stands out before Longstone Edge and high above the Manor House. Close by is another example of a typical local barn.

Orr's Barn as it was before conversion. The initials on the centre pillar stand for Thomas Gregory Orr who was born in Litton in 1807 and died 3 April 1881, in Great Longstone. He was a farmer of 350 acres of land, and a cheese factor.

LITTLE LONGSTONE CONGREGATIONAL CHAPEL

The Reverend Malkin Mills was a popular Vicar of Great Longstone and the people were said to be "eminently blessed by the labours and example of a pious Clergyman". When he moved elsewhere, his successor was quickly shunned by a group of people who were unhappy with his religious persuasion (he was High Church). His teaching was described as so distasteful that the "thinking and pious" section of the congregation all became Independents or Congregationalists as they would now be called. They first moved to the Baptist Chapel on Ashford Lane and then, in June 1844, the foundation stone of their own chapel was laid by James Longsdon Esquire "in the midst of a large number of attentive spectators". It became the social centre of the village, not only offering a weekly church service but also such events as Penny Readings, which were a series of songs, piano recitals, poems and stories of an improving character. They were said to be free of "moral taint" and also highly amusing and instructive, the organizers believing that time is misspent unless there is some useful lesson to be learnt.

Karen Frenkel

Michael Stuart

LITTLE LONGSTONE CLUB AND READING ROOM

The Institute is the second building from the left (now an open space), between Parva and Christmas Cottages; on the opposite side of the road is Kath's garden. Note the ice-cream vans belonging to Peak Ices, one in the pinfold and another in front of the factory, lower far right.

Once upon a time, Little Longstone, just like big brother Great but not perhaps as grand, had a village hall known as the Institute. It wasn't built in stone, but it did provide warmth and shelter and entertainment for the people of the village and others from many miles around. It was first proposed in April 1922, and after discussion by the inevitable committee, a wooden building was purchased in 1924. It was re-erected on a concrete foundation and measured 70 feet by 18 feet. The total cost was £333.

At the opening, the chairman of the parish meeting, Mr. E. M. Longsdon, was reported to have said the Institute should be used not only for amusement and pleasure but also for something with real socialism about it, which was a bit rich, he being the chairman of the Bakewell Conservatives!

144 people then took part in a whist drive, followed by a dance; the Cressbrook Band gave their services free of charge. Whist drives and dances were most popular at first, the music being provided by Cressbrook Band, or by a Miss Mullins from Ashford, or by a monstrous gramophone, which needed two men to carry it. The next acquisition was a billiard table and it was not long before competitive matches were arranged, for example against the Calver Reading Room. The Institute was used by many organizations, such as the Women's Institute, the Monsal Head Tennis Club, Longstone British Legion, the Unionist League and Longstone Horticultural Society. A dance was held in aid of Bakewell Cottage Hospital, and in 1929, a course of six lectures was given on *Great Britain as an Imperial Power,* and later a series of talks on *The Origin of the Earth.*

When the war came, the Institute was used first as a school for evacuee children (Columbia Picture Corporation from London, then, in 1941, Wright and Sons, leather merchants, bombed out of West Bar, Sheffield, took the place over as a factory for repairing boots and shoes, and stayed there till about 1946. When the Institute re-opened after the war, a sausage and potato supper was held with the sausages supplied by Mr. Stones, the potatoes and tea by Messrs. Nuttall and Bacon, cakes by Mr. Gilbert and milk by Mr. Timm, a truly cooperative venture. In 1950 the week was divided up between one night each for the cinema, Boy Scouts, children between six and eight years, billiards and a whist drive. It closed sometime in the 1970s.

David Fletcher (scroll)

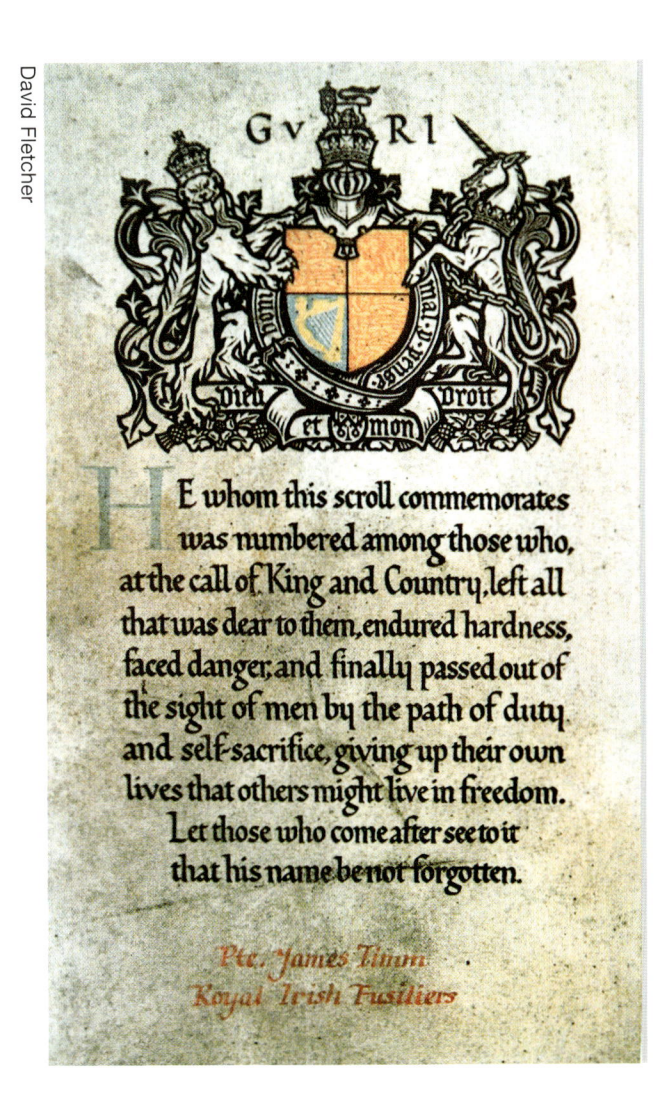

David Fletcher (photograph)

> HE whom this scroll commemorates was numbered among those who, at the call of King and Country, left all that was dear to them, endured hardness, faced danger, and finally passed out of the sight of men by the path of duty and self-sacrifice, giving up their own lives that others might live in freedom. Let those who come after see to it that his name be not forgotten.
>
> *Pte. James Timm*
> *Royal Irish Fusiliers*

Twenty men from Little Longstone took part in the Great War including two Bacons, two Timms and three Luptons. Five of the twenty were awarded disablement pensions, and Fred Cowan Slack and James Renwick Timm were both killed in action. In the Second World War, James's nephew, also James Renwick Timm, was killed in Italy in 1944. Their memorials can be seen inside the chapel porch. The above photographs show James Timm in his uniform as a private in the Royal Irish Fusiliers, and the certificate sent to his grieving parents on his death.

Walter Adamson

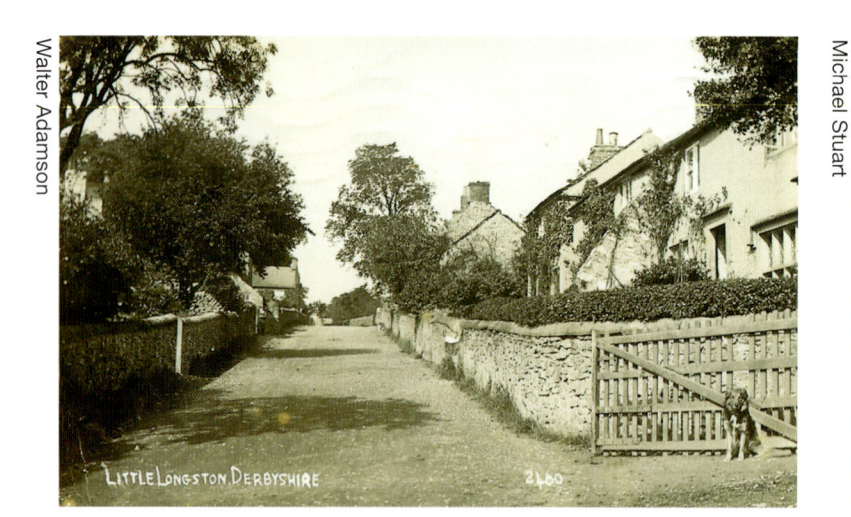

Michael Stuart

Walter Adamson

Walter Adamson

These four photographs, taken from postcards, show Main Street at various dates before 1914, from Holly Tree to Monsal Head. The man with the horse and cart is John Timm, the local general-purpose carter and carrier.

Noel Green

Karen Frenkel

The Stocks photographed in the early 20th century and again after renovation in 2000.

THE STOCKS

Now called the Stocks, but known as Fynney Cottage in Victorian times, this is believed to be the oldest house in the village, as you can see by the date-stone high up in the gable end - 1575 and I F for James or John Fynney. More important than that, inside the house are two pairs of crucks, a cruck being two curved timbers joined together to support the roof, showing that the house was originally timber-framed, probably with wattle-and-daub infilling, and not stone walled as it is now. James Fynney was born on 2 March 1596, and after marrying Mary, the daughter of Ralph White of Ashford, they both settled in Little Longstone. Thomas Longsdon gent, born 7 October 1677, at Armley near Leeds, married Elizabeth daughter of William Fynney senior of Little Longstone on 27 October 1702 and was buried on 10 March 1737/8 at Great Longstone. The will of the last Fynney of Little Longstone, William by name, is dated 24 April 1749.

The Gardener's Cottage next door may have been the kitchen to the Stocks; the large open fire necessary for cooking vast quantities of food for guests and servants was often kept separate from the main dwelling to prevent the possible spread of fire.

Near the Stocks are the actual stocks, the symbol of authority, and the place where justice was dispensed. In the spinney, on the opposite side of the road, is the village well and just below, in the field, are the visible remains of three fishponds. The first pinfold, or pound, where straying livestock were kept, is next to the well. The later pinfold is opposite Noel's house.

THE MANOR

In 1661 Bernard White, a Great Longstone Merchant, rented the "mansion house" in which he then lived, for £43 a year from Elizabeth Longsdon of Middlewood House, Bradfield, Yorkshire. He was required to pay all the taxes, not plough the land without her consent, keep the house in good repair, and collect the rents due to Elizabeth from her tenants. At the same time he also rented the Home Farm from the Wright family of Great Longstone.

There is a story that, during the Civil War, Elizabeth was watching, from a safe place, a battle between Roundheads and Cavaliers near Sheffield, when she saw her husband Thomas fall from his horse. She dashed into the midst of the slaughter, lifted him onto his horse and galloped away to the nearest infirmary. Then returning to the fray she led her husband's troop into battle and victory, and forever after was known as Captain Bess. Unfortunately, Thomas died, but two weeks later his widow successfully gave birth to a son, thus perpetuating a line stretching back to the Norman Conquest. Well, it *IS* only a story.

In 1700, the Manor was built, or re-built, by another Thomas Longsdon who was born in Armley near Leeds, but for that period it is small and old-fashioned, perhaps because that was all he could afford. He spent over £20 on works including repairs to floors, partitions, chimneys, a staircase, the building of at least one extension and a coat of arms on a chimneypiece.

The Manor and its garden, home to Jim, Michelle and Alexander.

Michelle, holding the youngest arrival in the village, Alexander James, and Jim.

JAMES LONGSDON (1745-1821)

The Longsdon family made their money out of sheep and cattle, but James, who was a member of the circle of business and social friends hovering around Sir Richard Arkwright, the entrepreneur of the Derbyshire cotton spinning industry, decided to try something different. About 1787, he built his own cotton mill which was powered not by wind or water, and certainly not by steam, but by a horse! He also built or acquired two warehouses and a weaving shed, all in Great Longstone. They sold the finished products to America and Russia and other countries, but by the time of the Napoleonic Wars, Britain had blockaded the Continent, and America in return had forbidden trading with Britain, so a financial crisis then arose both generally and within the company. According to Francis Tomes, the entire Longsdon property was about to be sold to meet the demands of creditors, when William, James's son, returned in 1828 from his prosperous business in America and purchased the estate.

ERNEST MOREWOOD LONGSDON (1867-1940)

He was a local architect who designed and constructed a number of buildings in Derbyshire, including the Infirmary and Vagrants Ward of the Bakewell Workhouse, now Newholme Hospital, and the Post Office in Bakewell. He was also secretary of the Bakewell Centre for Technical Education, and of Bakewell Town Hall Co., and actuary to Bakewell Savings Bank. He left the estate to his nephew, Geoffrey, leaving his son Anthony as tenant for life. When Tony died, the estate reverted to Geoffrey's daughter Joan, and she passed it on to the son of her sister, Elizabeth Warman. Thus it was, that Joan, Mary and Jim arrived in Little Longstone, and Jim made the Manor House his home, and assumed the name of Longsdon

Michael Stuart

Karen Frenkel

Karen Frenkel

The Packhorse in the early 1900s was very much the same as today.

Mine host Robert observes the antics of his customers with a "seen it all before" grin.

THE PACKHORSE INN

The earliest evidence we have for an inn in the village is a document which records that on 4 August, 1787, William Goodwin sold a house, barn, cowhouse and garden to John Ashton of Rowland for £50. It passed to the Hewitt family by marriage, and was sold to William Taylor in 1869 for £200. William, as well as being a publican, was also a lead miner and general labourer, an extreme case of moonlighting. It was finally sold in 1931 for £800 to Marston, Thompson and Evershed whose successors still own what is now the social centre of the village. Was it called the Packhorse because it was on a route used by packhorses? Maybe, but in 1306 there lived in Little Longstone a man called Thomas le Jager, and a jager or jagger was a man in charge of packhorses which carried ore from the lead mines to the smelter. George Hulley or Hooley is listed as a licensed victualler in 1777 and 1778, and William Longsdon as an alehouse keeper as far back as 1577, but that establishment could have been in Great Longstone.

Karen Frenkel

COMMITTEE MEETING

This panoramic view shows just one of the many meetings held to discuss the millennium book in the salubrious and convivial atmosphere of the Packhorse Inn.

(Left to right) Pam, Hylda, Noel, Kate, Ann, Peter, Alison, Mike, Jim, Dan, Sam, Sarah, Walter, Dick, Robert, Ray, Annie, and Mark.

We have to thank in particular the Lorains family, Pam, Kate, Mary and Martha, for starting the ball rolling, as it were, by distributing questionnaires to all the inhabitants in the parish and then collating them (the results were more interesting than the electoral roll). Sadly Pam died before she could see the results of her pioneering efforts.

Michael Stuart

Peter Davey

The Outrake, early 20th century and as it is now (above), and the former stables (below).

Karen Frenkel

THE OUTRAKE

The Outrake was built before 1814 and was owned and occupied by the Longsdon family as a sort of dower house, a place where the old folks were sent when the younger generation took charge of things. It was later used by their friends, the Morewoods of Thornbridge, and also by the Shaws who purchased it in about 1870. In the 1920s it became a monastery and then a holiday cottage during the summer months for the Arning family of Manchester. Their gardener kept them well supplied with fruit and veg, whether they were in residence or not. When they were away, the village lads used the snooker room as an unofficial youth club, and during the war evacuees from Ashgate, Chesterfield, occupied it as a children's home. Derbyshire Social Services then used it for the same purpose before the house reverted once again to private ownership. The stables and barns have also been converted into comfortable houses.

Castle Cliffe House and Sally (or is it Lottie?).

Monsal Head Hotel.

Alan.

Kate and Mary.

TV Star Chris Evans and Liz.

The Monsal Head Hotel, or Bull's Head as it used to be called, is referred to in a directory of 1835, but it was certainly in existence in 1783. Margaret Holmes was landlady for 44 years, her son Joseph for 25 years. It was described as a quaint and old hostling, beautified and ornamented in 1883, new stables were added in 1885, and the hotel re-built in 1887. Monsal Head Café was built for the navvies during the construction of the railway in 1860, and had a front wall made of timber planking, and a roof of corrugated iron. Inside the front door was a desk where the men who worked on the railway were paid. There was also an inn at Nether Dale Farm, where one Robert Shaw was listed as a licensed innkeeper in 1753.

1 Tom Richardson was water bailiff for Chatsworth for many years. His wife Margaret was a much-loved teacher at Great Longstone who never forgot the children she taught, nor they her.

2 Stephen, the water bailiff, in Monsal Dale with a friend.

3/4 Monsal Dale in the monsoon season. Upper Dale and Nether Dale.

Monsal Dale station was opened in 1866, three years after the completion of the railway. Unfortunately, the only method of crossing the river was by way of stepping stones at Upper Dale, a rather dangerous undertaking particularly in winter. In spite of heart-rending pleas by the inhabitants, the Midland Railway would do nothing, so a footbridge was provided in 1870 by public subscription, Mr. McConnell of Cressbrook Mill donating several larch trees. A cart bridge would have to wait till the next century.

1. The cart bridge in front of Dean Cottage and Cosy Cottage.
2. Cows grazing by the River Wye under the exposed limestone of White Cliff.
3. June, David and John Clarke outside Upperdale House.
4. Michael and Loreen Isherwood were married at Cressbrook Church in September 2000.
5. Upper Dale from an old postcard. Note the footbridge and the road swinging round to approach the ford.

27

Left, Water-cum-Jolly and right, Cressbrook Mill.

The parish boundary between Little Longstone and Cressbrook runs, strangely enough, down the middle of Cressbrook Dale, does a u-turn directly in front of Cressbrook Mill and disappears up the River Wye and across the middle of the lake in Water-cum-Jolly, half of which is therefore in the parish. Anyway, it's a good excuse for some delightful pictures.

Karen Frenkel

Karen Frenkel

1 The Wye is fished by local men and those who come from afar. Here fly fisherman and author John Cawthorne and friend Wilf tackle the trout.

2 The Weir downstream from the viaduct in Monsal Dale.

Although Cressbrook (once known as Grassbrook) is just outside the parish boundary, the mills and village are a very significant feature in the landscape, sitting as they do in the higher reaches of Upperdale at the division between the Wye valley and Ravensdale. It was here, in the 1780s, that Richard Arkwright built a mill with a dam across the Cress Brook to provide the necessary power. In 1814, after a dam was built to form the lake in Water-cum-Jolly, William Newton constructed the so-called Big Mill (the one with the bell tower) which used water from the River Wye. The buildings to house the apprentices and the 1878 school can be seen above the mill. He had also erected the cottages at Ravensdale to accommodate his workers.

Henry, James and William McConnel, otherwise known as McConnel and Company of Manchester, bought the mills in 1835 and completely changed the area, building Cressbrook Hall, and most of the houses in the village, soon after that date.

Noel feeding the horses from his garden, walking in Main Street and somewhere in Europe during the war.

NOEL GREEN

Noel was born 80 years ago in the cottage now called Meadow View. When Noel was five years old, the family moved to Parva Cottage and he has been there ever since, apart from his war service. Leaving school at the age of 14, he worked for Harry Shaw at his Great Longstone garage, for five shillings a week, but a week later he bought a lawn-mower from Harry for five bob, which he still has, so he ended up with no cash. He was later employed driving a lorry full of spar down from Longstone Edge to Hassop Station. When the war came, he first volunteered for the Home Guard. In 1941 he joined up at what is now the Ashgate Hospice, which had been taken over by the army for the duration. Noel became a member of the Guards Armoured Division at Warminster, driving a troop carrier containing 32 men; training on Salisbury Plain and later on the Yorkshire moors. Then loading up at the West India docks in London, he landed at Arromanches six days after D-Day, passing through Caen to eventually help to liberate Brussels on his birthday in September 1944. He was once ordered to drive his vehicle round a field to make sure no mines had been planted there! After taking part in the attempt to aid the paratroops at Arnheim, and assisting the Americans in the Ardennes, Noel and his comrades finally reached Germany, being stationed in Cologne, Berlin, Hamburg and Kiel. He left by ship from Cuxhaven, preceded by an icebreaker, and landed in Hull where he was demobilised in 1947, and returned to Little Longstone where he has been ever since.

Alison with Robertson and Michael with Finn, outside Christmas Cottage.

Christmas Cottage goes back to at least 1700 when it belonged to a William Tattershall whose occupation was seriously set down as rabbit catcher. It then was sold to Joshua Barton, a farmer in a small way, who handed it on to his son Joseph, framework knitter, who in turn sold it to Martin Furness, carpenter. His nephew Joseph, shoemaker, (it seems everybody had a different trade in the village in those days) built a small house next door. At some stage the two houses were joined together and later purchased by the Nuttall family, (ancestors of Dorothy Adamson). The bit that sticks out at the end was called Harlem and has at various times been a carpenter's shop, undertaker's establishment, and a doss-house (at 2/6d [12.5p] a night, bring your own bed).

Roger Cox

Karen Frenkel

Walter seems to spend most days catching the bus to somewhere or other. As his son Keith said, "He's got more of a social life than me."

WALTER AND DOROTHY ADAMSON

Walter came from the village of Beighton, once in Derbyshire, now part of Sheffield, also famous as the home of the Queen of the Gypsies. He started his working life at Waleswood Colliery, and although he reported to Eckington for a medical to join the Corps of Transport, he was turned down, not because he was medically unfit, but because he was, as a miner, in a reserved occupation. Dorothy was born the same year as Walter, 1918, in Little Longstone, and worked at Cressbrook when it was a working cotton mill. During the war she was employed in the NAAFI at the army camp in Bakewell, near to Burton Closes. Walter was a keen cyclist, and often camped at White Lodge. One day he went into the Bull's Head at Ashford and there he met Dorothy, and his long distance cycling days were over, They were married at the chapel in August 1947, and Walter moved to the house which had been in Dorothy's family since 1816, and where she lived with her father, Henry Nuttall. Incidentally, when Henry was a lad, he had to collect water from the troughs opposite the Packhorse, and carry it in a bucket to a barn at the far end of Chapel Lane, where the cows were waiting to be watered. Walter first of all worked for the council, and one of his first jobs was to make the footpath, which we all use between the chapel and Monsal Head. He moved to Furniss and Hassall, the builders of Great Longstone, and then to Sellors of Bakewell, also builders, before he finished his career at Glebe Mines, up on Longstone Moor. At some time he also drove a lorry, but as he didn't have a licence, he gave it up before he was caught out. He was a natural roofer, and you can't get far in Derbyshire before you come upon a roof that Walter had a hand in at some time. He was once half way up the Hunting Tower at Chatsworth, when his mate said, "Do you think you ought to put a safety harness on, Walter?" On another occasion, Malcolm Sellors held on to him while he dangled over the edge of Edensor Institute roof, inspecting the gutter. Sadly Dorothy passed away a few years ago but we are reminded of her by one of her poems printed here.

A DERBYSHIRE DALE

They all come here to see the view
On foot by car and cycle too.
In summer sun and autumn haze
They all come here to browse and gaze.
Trains ran through here years ago.
We wish them back, but even so
With God's good grace we have this vale.
This beauteous, lovely Monsal Dale

Dorothy Margaret Adamson 1918-1998

Dorothy and Angus.

This photograph, taken in the grounds of nearby Thornbridge Hall in 1916, shows the guests at the wedding of Mary Ann Taylor to Ernest Edward Gilbert, son of Isiah Gilbert. The bride, who was the game cook at Thornbridge, and groom, are at the centre of the front row. To the left is Sarah Ann Gilbert, Noel Green's grandmother. Noel's grandfather Isiah, to the right of the groom, first worked with horses and drugs (carts not aspirins) and later as a ganger on the railway line between Longstone and Hassop. He was, however, most famous for his topiary (the clipping of hedges into fantastic shapes) and speeding passengers would gaze with amazement at the birds, animals and other wondrous shapes he created. The child at the front is Noel's sister Cecily, and her mother Rossellen is fourth from the left at the back. The tall man to the centre rear is Fred Slack, who died in the Great War.

One of the old industries of Little Longstone was basket making. Henry Nuttall, Dorothy Adamson's father, had a workshop behind Sunnyside (now Max's garage) and he was a basket maker for a number of cotton mills, including Cressbrook, Litton and Belper. He gave up the work because his customers didn't pay on time giving him what we now call cashflow problems.

Noel Green

Walter Adamson

Ray Manley

Mary Longsdon

Karen Frenkel

1 Norma and her dogs after a long walk up the Edge.

2 Tom, Norma, and Isabelle relaxing after a hard day.

3 Isabelle and friend (Zorro or Golly Miss Molly?).

1 Libby in the Packhorse.

2 Robert gets his supply of fresh meat from Fred Mellor, the butcher from Great Longstone.

3 The school bus arrives and another day begins for the scholars of Lady Manners in Bakewell.

4 Jane, Tilly, Jack and Amey.

5 Bill and friends.

6 The flower bedecked cottage of David and Sheila.

7 Kath and her lovely garden in which she spends so much time.

37

Ray Manley

Jim Longsdon

Karen Frenkel

Karen Frenkel

Horses are once again a common sight in the Village.

When we first saw Mary trudging up the road with a bale of hay on her back to feed the horses, and her sister Joan in her van with what looked like half the dogs in the village, we knew they were going to fit in nicely.

1 Mary's house, The Eaglets. This was formerly a shop owned by Mrs. Maltby and her daughter Jane. It was rather unusual in that the customers weren't allowed inside. Instead they had to knock on the door, which would then be opened by Jane, and then they would shout their orders to the mother who sat inside on a chair.

2 Mary and just two of her ponies.

3 Joan and the dogs.

1 Ray and Daphne.

2 If you look carefully, you can see Liz, the head gardener in her wonderful garden.

3 Karina and Harry.

4 No, Mike and Liz are not waiting for a bus, or the pub to open, they're staring in amazement at the well-dressing.

Peter Wrench

Karen Frenkel

1 Suzy Wrench, and Matthias Guterl of Waldfischbach Germany, were married In St. Giles, Great Longstone in June 1998, And you can see they had a wonderful, sunny day for the reception in a marquee in front of Longstone Byre.

2 At Longstone Byre, continuing the ancient tradition of dry stone walling.

1   An Australian wearing a kilt must be a rare sight!

2   Another sunny day, this time for the wedding, in the chapel, of Olivia Stuart, spinster of this parish, and Andrew Lovett of Woolongong, Australia.

3   The Rev. Nicola Jones made sure it was not only a solemn occasion, but also a fun day.

1 The postman Stuart Chatfield, has associations with Little Longstone apart from delivering the morning post to a still-sleeping village. His great grandparents, James and Elizabeth Andrews lived here and are buried in the chapel-yard, and his great aunt, Marie Franks lived in Hope Cottage.

2 The post-box at Monsal Head, set in a typical dry-stone wall, green fields behind, and blue sky above Longstone Edge. Others are at Upper Dale and next to the Hollow.

3 Did you know there used to be a pond in the middle of the village between The Hollow and Home Farm? It was called the Mere and was filled in as a "public nuisance and prejudicial to health." In return, William Longsdon put in the pump and troughs for £15, at his own expense, for the use of the village. They were repaired before the first well-dressing, about ten years ago.

Karen Frenkel

Brian Edwards

Karen Frenkel

Karen Frenkel

44

1 This photograph was taken when the large field by Nether Dale Farm was being used for filming an episode of the television series "Peak Practice".

2 Every Wednesday evening at the Packhorse is Folk Night, a jolly occasion when it's difficult to find a seat.

The Peak District has been a favourite area for serious ramblers for many years, and consequently the public footpaths are well signposted (how nice to see not only the destination marked, but also how far it is), such as this example next to the Packhorse. Of course you can have a meal and a swift pint or two of Pedigree before you go, or you can stroll up to Monsal Head, admiring the colourful gardens on the way, and admire the view while you sample an ice-cream. If you prefer the footpath to Great Longstone, you could find yourself trying to negotiate the "squeezers", described as such for obvious reasons.

Winter in Little Longstone with a covering of snow is a magical wonderland, and these photographs, from different sources, I think proves it.

1 Across the traditional sledging slope with the Hollow and Manor House in the middle distance.

2 The Packhorse, a beacon of light in the snow.

3 Main Street with Dean Cottage and Hope Cottage on the left.

4 A view taken from behind the Manor, with Holly Tree to the left and Parva to the right.

Monsal Dale from two different perspectives.

1 The Outrake, now divided into Outrake House on the left, and Chestnut House on the right, with Chris standing in front of her portion.

2 Very appropriate!

3 The quaintly named, Water-cum-Jolly.
   Half the lake is in Cressbrook, half in Little Longstone.

A study in autumn leaves, some with a touch of frost.

49

1. Spring is on the way, with the daffodils planted by the village in the foreground, Christmas Cottage in the distance.

2. Meadow Cranesbill.

3. Saxifrage.

4. Burnet moth on Scabious flower.

WELL DRESSING

No one knows how old well dressing is in Derbyshire or anywhere else, but everyone can speculate. It may date back to the Celts who certainly had a thing about rivers and lakes, depositing all kinds of treasure in what were presumably special locations. Buxton, an ancient spa town, is a good case. Named by the Romans after a Celtic goddess, Arnemetiae, Roman coins and three bronze bracelets were found in the hot springs where the Romans luxuriated themselves.

Stage 1. First take your boards (and these are no lightweights, even when dry), and soak them in the river for two weeks.

Stage 2. Remove boards from river, preferably keeping water out of wellies.

51

Stage 3. Prepare the clay. This involves trampling in wet clay (the technical term is "puddling"), some people enjoy it, and some don't! These do.

Stage 4. The now thoroughly yukky clay is prepared and put on the boards.

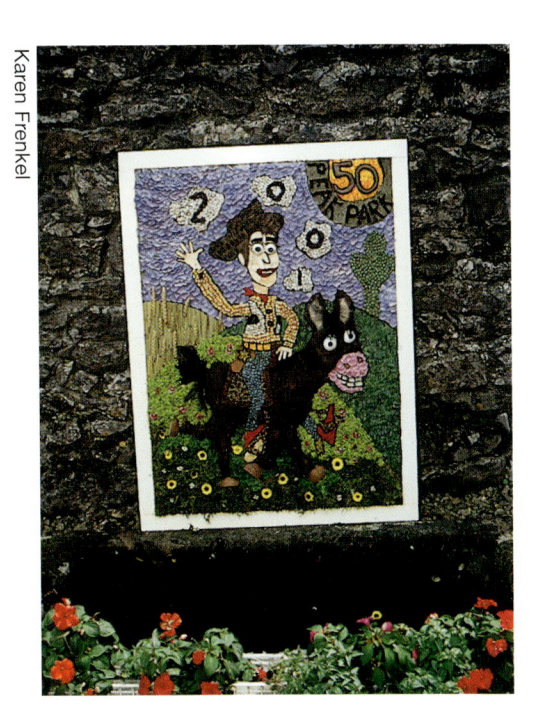

After the triumph of Christianity, Buxton became or remained a holy well. It was also a place of healing named after Saint Anne and those who were cured of their ailments left votive offerings, such as discarded crutches and clothing. Well dressing, as we know it, was first carried out in modern times at Tissington in 1615, a year when wells ran dry. It was revived sometime before 1758 and has since spread throughout the area.

Left: The children have their own well too.

Stage 5. Bring on the artists! The design is pricked through onto the clay, the outlines highlighted, and the natural material pressed into the clay.

Stage 6. Start building the superstructure. This is where we need one man (Jim) and his tractor, and Annie who isn't afraid of a bit of dirt. An appreciative audience gathers.

And here it is, the result of a lot of intricate planning and lots of hard work.

Karen Frenkel

Karen Frenkel

Karen Frenkel

Karen Frenkel

Karen Frenkel

The Blessing of the Well with plenty of interested spectators - some even bring their own chairs! Mark (left) and Peter, respectively chairman and treasurer of the Parish Meeting, have been very much involved with this publication.

55

The Fete Queen and her attendants came with the Rev. Clive Thrower. The Cressbrook Band played and young Robert entertained with his violin too.

Little Longstone Well Dressing 2001.

Karen Frenkel

Many of the residents turned out on this sunny morning in September 2001 for a group photograph in the field opposite the Manor.

Two Packhorse regulars from Great Longstone looked on, bemused.

Karen Frenkel

Hylda Fletcher

Just one of the many glorious sunsets over Monsal Head provides a fitting ending for this book. We hope you have enjoyed it.